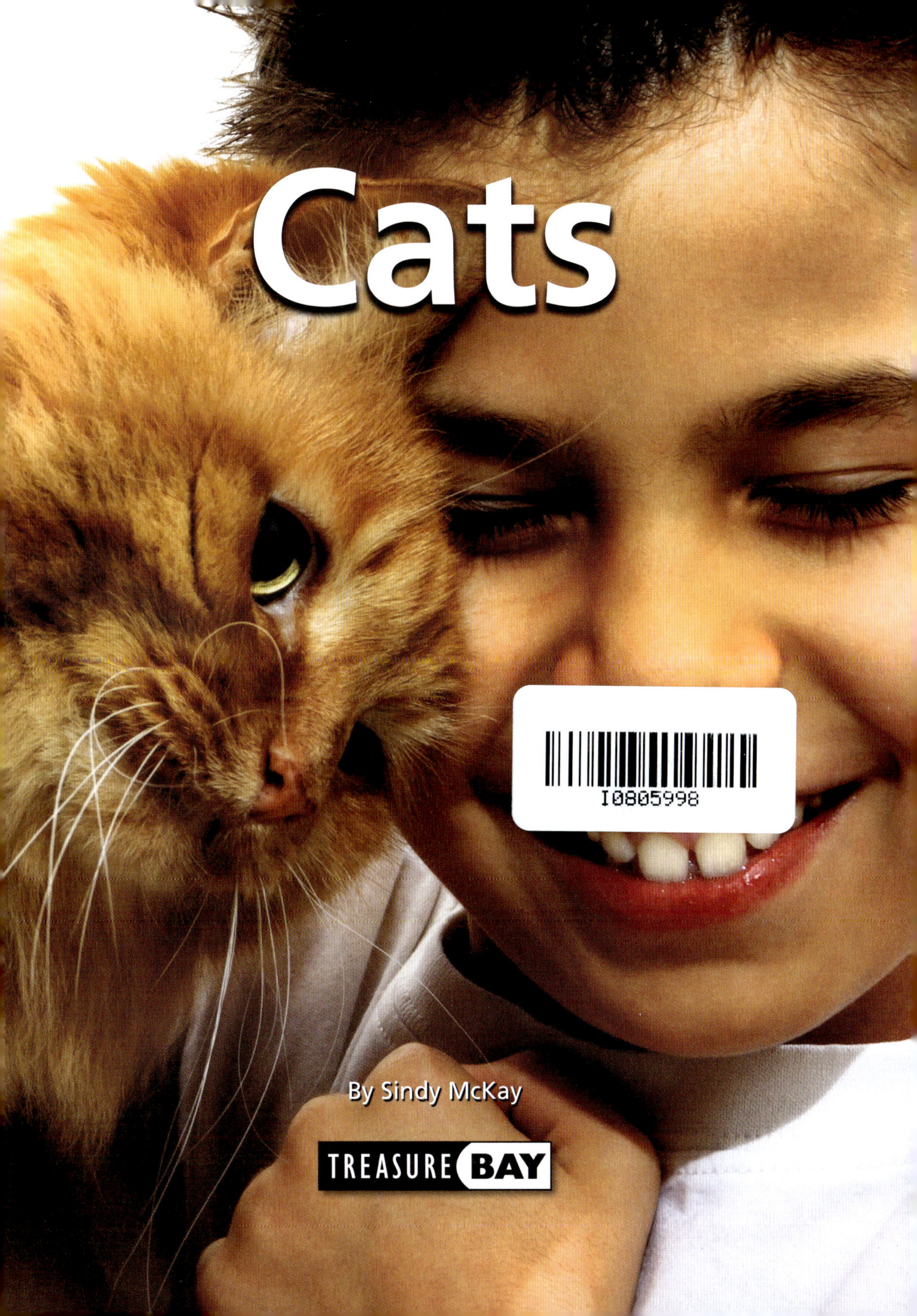

# Cats

By Sindy McKay

TREASURE BAY

WE BOTH READ®

# Parent's Introduction

**Whether your child is a beginning reader, a reluctant reader, or an eager reader, this book offers a fun and easy way to encourage and help your child in reading.**

Developed with reading education specialists, **We Both Read** books invite you and your child to take turns reading aloud. You read the left-hand pages of the book, and your child reads the right-hand pages—which have easier text written at a specific reading level. The result is a wonderful new reading experience and faster reading development!

You may find it helpful to read the entire book aloud yourself the first time, then invite your child to participate the second time. As you read, try to make the story come alive by reading with expression. This will help to model good fluency.

In some books, a few challenging words are introduced in the parent's text with **bold** lettering. Pointing out and discussing these words can help to build your child's reading vocabulary. If your child is a beginning reader, it may be helpful to run a finger under the text as each of you reads. To help show whose turn it is, a blue dot ● comes before text for you to read, and a red star ★ comes before text for your child to read.

If your child struggles with a word, you can encourage "sounding it out," but keep in mind that this will not help with all words because some words don't follow phonetic patterns.

You can help with breaking down the sounds of the letters or syllables, but if your child becomes too frustrated, it is usually best to simply say the word.

While reading together, try to help your child understand what is being read. It can help to stop every few pages to ask questions about the text and check if there are any words your child doesn't understand. After you finish the book, ask a few more questions or discuss what you've read together. Rereading this book multiple times may also help your child to read with more ease and understanding.

Most importantly, remember to praise your child's efforts and keep the reading fun. Keep the tips above in mind, but don't worry about doing everything right. Simply sharing the enjoyment of reading together will increase your child's reading skills and help to start your child on a lifetime of reading enjoyment!

**Cats**

A We Both Read® Book: Level 1
Guided Reading: Level E

---





Published by
Treasure Bay, Inc.
PO Box 519
Roseville, CA 95661 USA

Printed in China

Library of Congress Control Number: 2024910006

ISBN: 978-1-60115-379-1

Visit us online at:
**WeBothRead.com**

PR-10-24

# Table of Contents

# WHAT IS A CAT?

- Cats are amazing, beautiful animals. Wild cats, however, can be very dangerous. They do not make **great** pets. Lucky for humans, there are also tame, or **domestic**, cats.

★ **Domestic** cats make **great** pets!

- **Many**, many years ago all cats were wild. However, domestic cats have now been around for nearly ten thousand years. Today, cats are one of the most popular pets in the world and **many people** have them in their homes.

★ Some **people** think cats make the best pets. Some people think dogs are the best. **Many** people like both cats AND dogs!

- Domestic cats are often called house cats. **They** are the perfect pet to keep indoors. Most cats quickly learn to use a litter box for their bathroom. **They** easily entertain themselves with cat toys.

★ Cats can sleep 14 hours a day. **They** like to nap in the sun.

- Cats love to climb. Many cat owners have a **fancy** climbing tree for their cats to play on.

★ Cat toys do not have to be **fancy**. A box makes a great toy for a cat.

- Cats have a strong instinct to **scratch**. It helps to keep their claws sharp. It also expresses emotions, like excitement or stress. Many cat owners have a special post for their cat to **scratch**.

★ To **scratch** a post is good.
To scratch a chair is not good!

- A young cat is called a kitten. Kittens love to play! Playing is how they learn. One of their favorite games is "hide and **pounce**."

★ A kitten will hide. It will wait for something to pass. Then it will **pounce**!

- Cats and kittens enjoy playing with dangling toys and soft balls. Playing with bubbles is also fun.

★ Even a pen can be a toy to a cat!

- Most kittens are fast learners. It doesn't take long to train them to use a litter box or a scratching post.

★ But most of the time they just want to play!

# TAKING CARE OF A CAT

- It may be that cats are such popular pets because they are very independent. This can make them easier to care for than pets who need more of an owner's attention. Any pet, however, has certain needs to keep them healthy and **happy**.

★ All cats need fresh water and good cat food. A well-fed cat is a **happy** cat.

- It's **also** important for pets to have regular visits to the doctor to check on their health. Pet doctors, called veterinarians, help to keep cats healthy by vaccinating them against major cat diseases.

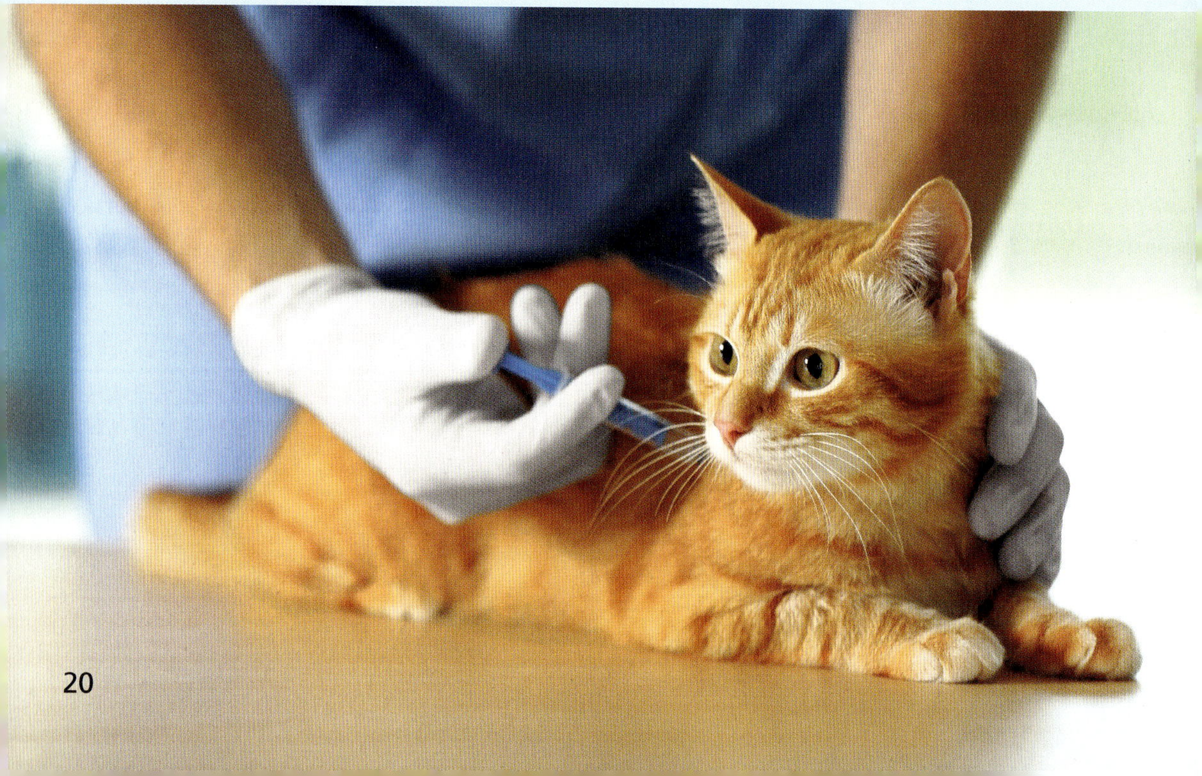

★ A vet can **also** help when a cat gets sick. The vet can help the cat feel better.

- Cats don't seem to mind being left home alone all day. But it is important to **know** that your cat needs attention and affection when you return. All cats are different, and some need more attention than others.

★ Your cat will let you **know** what it needs.

# CAT COMMUNICATION

- Cats communicate in many ways. They make a variety of noises, and each one means something different. A loud meow usually means they want you to pay attention! Or you may hear your cat **purr**.

★ Your cat may **purr** when you pet it. A cat that purrs is a happy cat.

- A cat may use its ears to communicate. When its ears are forward, that means the cat is interested in something. Ears back means they are **scared**. Ears to the side means they are mad.

★ A cat's back may go up. This means it is mad or **scared**. It may also hiss.

- Cats can be very patient. Most will let you carry them, play with them, and sleep with them. But, just like humans, sometimes they are just not in the mood. Listen to your cat. When it tells you it is unhappy, leave it alone.

★ If a cat has its back up—step away. Or you may get a scratch or a bite!

# CAT BREEDS

Bengal

Himalayan

Siamese



- There are many different breeds of cat that make wonderful pets.

A Himalayan *(him-uh-LAY-un)* Siamese cat has **beautiful** long hair. Another breed of Siamese has short hair.

★ Both breeds have **beautiful** blue eyes.

Russian Blue

- Russian Blue cats have an unusual eye color. Their eyes are a stunning blue-green that is rarely seen in any other animal. Norwegian *(nor-WEE-jen)* forest cats have green, gold, copper, or blue eyes.

Norwegian Forest

Abyssinian

Scottish Fold

★ Some cat breeds have big ears. Some cat breeds have small ears.

Scottish Fold

Savannah

Singapura

- Singapura (*sing-ah-PUR-ah*) is the smallest breed of domestic cat. A **purebred** Singapura is about half the size of a normal cat.

  The largest breed is the Maine coon. This cat can weigh as much as a big watermelon.

Maine Coon

★ **Purebred** cats are beautiful. But most cats are a mix of breeds. Many people think mixed-breed cats make the best pets.

Cats are **amazing** animals in many ways. They have an extraordinary sense of smell. The bumps and ridges on a cat's nose are as unique as a human's fingerprint, and no two noses are exactly the same.

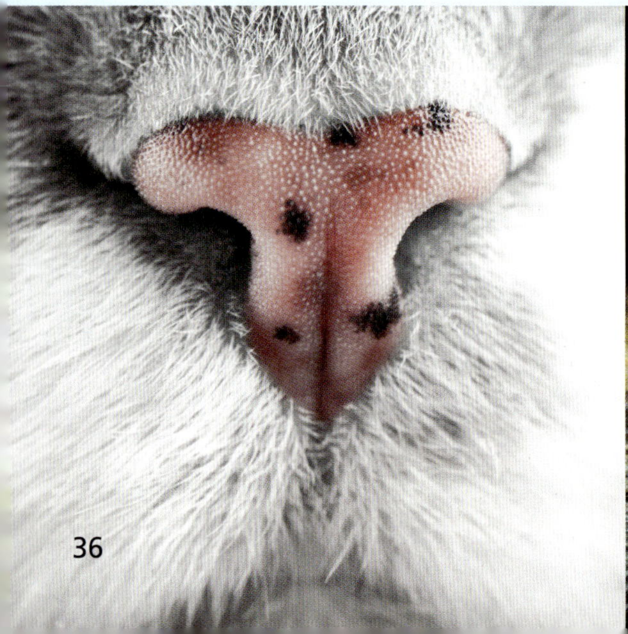

★ The eyes of a cat are also **amazing**. They can see things in very low light.

- The whiskers on a cat are very useful. They stick out from the face and feel the objects around them. This helps the cat avoid bumping into things when it's dark.

Cats see and smell very well, but what about **taste**?

★ Cats can **taste** most things. But they can't taste things that are sweet!

- Here is one last **awesome** fact about cats. They can be taught to do fun tricks, like sit, come, fetch, and "high five." Some cats have even learned how to open doors.

★ No wonder so many people have pet cats. Cats are **awesome**!

# Glossary

**communicate**
expressing thoughts and feeling to others

**domestic**
living with humans instead of living in the wild

**independent**
able to take care of oneself

**instinct**
natural behavior that an animal is born with and does not need to be taught

**purebred**
having ancestors that are all the same breed of animal

**veterinarian**
doctor for animals, also called a vet

# Questions to Ask after Reading

Add to the benefits of reading this book by discussing answers to these questions. Also consider discussing a few of your own questions.

1. What are some of the differences between a domestic animal and a wild animal?

2. What are some of the ways that cats communicate? What are some things they might be expressing?

3. Why do you think it's important to get to know your cat?

4. Do you think it would be easy to teach a cat to do tricks? Why or why not?

5. Some people prefer cats and some people prefer dogs. Which do you like better and why?

If you liked ***Cats***, here are some other
We Both Read® books you are sure to enjoy!

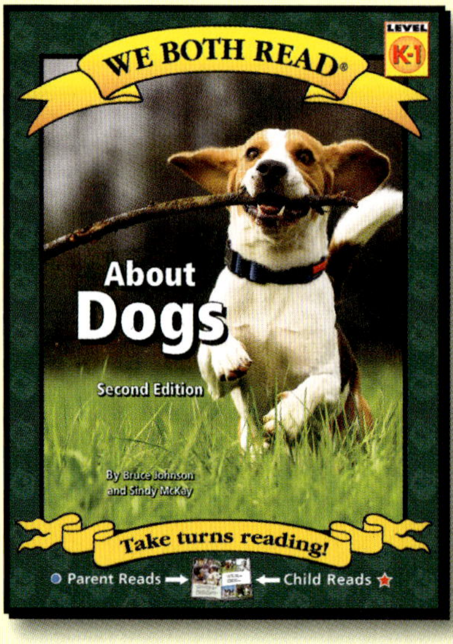


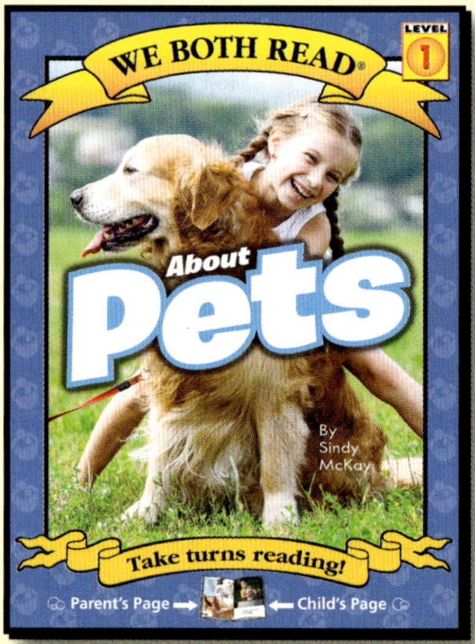


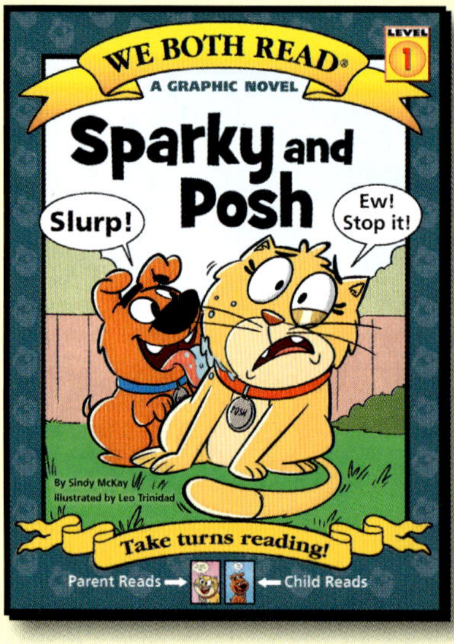


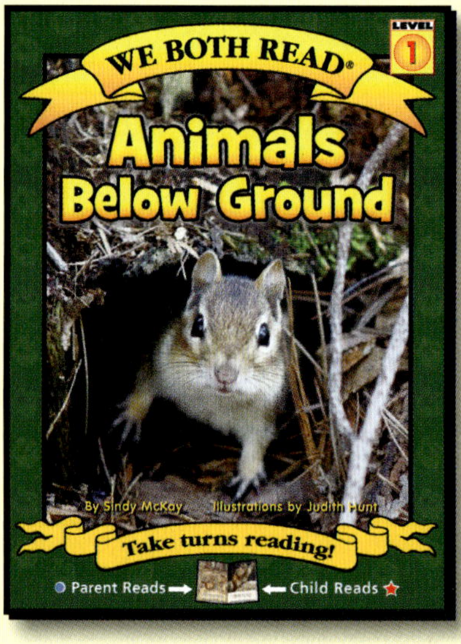


To see all the *We Both Read®* books that are available,
just go online to **WeBothRead.com**.